Author of *Leadership From Behind the Scenes*

DR. RON WEBB

EXPOSING THE ENEMY FROM BEHIND THE SCENES

CHALFANT ECKERT

PUBLISHING

Bob Bishop

EXPOSING THE ENEMY FROM BEHIND THE SCENES

Exposing the Enemy from Behind the Scenes

Library of Congress Control Number: 2016937887

ISBN: 978-1-63308-228-1 Hardback
978-1-63308-229-8 Paperback
978-1-63308-230-4 Digital

Interior and Cover Design by R'tor John D. Maghuyop

1028 S Bishop Avenue, Dept. 178
Rolla, MO 65401

Printed in United States of America

TABLE OF CONTENTS

FOREWORD

Christians struggle with sin. They are not exempt from temptations and human weaknesses that beset us all. The difference is in the handling. Christians have a rule book to play by that defines all situations and gives instructions on how to play by God's rules. That book, of course, is God's Word, *The Holy Bible*. Its pages contain the stories and examples of Godly men and women who overcame trials and tribulations without letting negative emotions and spirits overwhelm them and change their God-given personalities and destinies.

Dr. Ron Webb addresses the negative spirits in his typical *full-speed-ahead, no-holds-barred* manner and gives hope to those who struggle to overcome the negative influences that hold them hostage to mediocre lives of majoring in the minors and trivial pursuits. Instead, Bishop Webb exposes the negative spirits we struggle with and encourages us to grab the reins and charge ahead for the Kingdom, leaving the negative spirits to eat our dust.

You will enjoy this book and come away with a fresh Biblical perspective about handling the negatives so that people see Jesus when they watch you.

Dr. Kitty Bickford, DBS, CPC
Founder, Pasture Valley Children Missions
Founder, BenevoLance
Author, *Nonprofit Touchdown*
and *Do Your Own Nonprofit* series

ACKNOWLEDGMENTS

To Georgia, my beautiful wife and helpmate for your constant support and encouragement in everything I do. And to my children Ronnie, Jacqueline (Jerrell, Sr.), Tony (Ramona), and two of the greatest grandsons in the world, Jerrell, Jr., and Jaxson. To my incredible staff and advisors, Dave, Jacqueline, and Jeanne: Thank you for all you do.

INTRODUCTION

In my book, *Destroying the Root of Racism*,[1] I mention how in the Old Testament watchmen were posted along the walls of the cities. Their job was to keep an eye out for any approaching danger and to sound the alarm should danger arise. At the first sign of trouble, the watchman would sound a trumpet so the people in the city could prepare to ward off the enemy when they arrived at the gates.

Where are our watchmen today? Christian leaders, *you (we)* are the watchmen. It's time for us to be on our guard—to be on the lookout during these dangerous times, and to sound the trumpet of alarm as we prepare the people to fight the enemy!

"But if the watchman see the sword come, and blow not the trumpet, and the people be not warned; if the sword come, and take any person from among them, he is taken away in his iniquity; but his blood will I require at the watchman's hand." (Ezekiel 33:6).

As leaders, our God-appointed job is to warn the people of danger, and with that job comes a warning: If we fail to sound the alarm, the blood of the people will be on our hands. However, if we do warn them, and they refuse to listen, our hands are clean. We've done our job; the rest is up to them.

---

1 Dr. Ron Webb, Destroying the Root of Racism (Chalfant Eckert Publishing, Rolla, MO ©2015) page 55

"His watchmen are blind: they are all ignorant, they are all dumb dogs, they cannot bark; sleeping, lying down, loving to slumber." (Isaiah 56:10).

I believe there are too many silent leaders today. Isaiah called them dumb dogs that can't bark. Or in some cases, won't bark. As leaders, we are essentially the guard dogs of the Church. Our bark is meant to alert the Church to danger or run a thief out of our neighborhood. We are there to expose evil before it can take root and grow.

This book exposes many of the evil spirits used by the enemy to derail, sidetrack, and afflict God's family. I am sounding the alarm as the watchman, and I am praying that you listen and take heed.

Dr. Ron Webb

A CALL TO DISCERNMENT

"But strong meat belongeth to them that are of full age, even those who by reason of use have their senses exercised to discern both good and evil."
—Hebrews 5:14

Spirits are alive and well in our day and age, just as they were in the Old Testament and in the days when Jesus walked the earth. A large part of Jesus' ministry was the casting out of demons and evil spirits. When Jesus was confronted by people who were possessed by demonic spirits, He exercised authority to remove them. Recall the story of the demoniac of Gadara:

> "And they arrived at the country of the Gadarenes, which is over against Galilee. And when he went forth to land, there met him out of the city a certain man, which had devils long time, and ware no clothes, neither abode in any house, but in the tombs.
>
> "When he saw Jesus, he cried out, and fell down before him, and with a loud voice said, 'What have I to do with thee, Jesus, thou Son of God most high? I beseech thee, torment me not'.
>
> "(For he had commanded the unclean spirit to come out of the man. For oftentimes it had caught him: and he was kept bound with chains and in fetters; and he brake the bands, and was driven of the devil into the wilderness.)

> "And Jesus asked him, saying, 'What is thy name?' And he said, 'Legion' because many devils were entered into him. And they besought him that he would not command them to go out into the deep.
>
> "And there was there an herd of many swine feeding on the mountain: and they besought him that he would suffer them to enter into them. And he suffered them.
>
> "Then went the devils out of the man, and entered into the swine: and the herd ran violently down a steep place into the lake, and were choked." (Luke 8:26–33).

Not even a pig wants to be controlled by Satan's spirits!

Jesus exercised discernment with this man, and the Bible tells us in John 14:12 that we can do the same works as Jesus—and greater works. Discernment is the supernatural ability to see beyond the physical in order to identify the spirits at work so we can know if they are angelic or demonic. It's the ability to see beyond those things that are false that gives us clarity to identify what is truly in the heart.

Discernment is a gift of the Holy Spirit.

"For to one is given by the Spirit the word of wisdom; to another the word of knowledge by the same Spirit; to another faith by the same Spirit; to another the gifts of healing by the same Spirit; to another the working of miracles; to another prophecy; **to another discerning of spirits**; to another divers kinds of tongues; to another the interpretation of tongues." (1 Corinthians 12:8–10, emphasis by author)

To properly perceive, distinguish, and recognize the spirits at work and expose the enemy from behind the scenes, we need the gift of discernment.

CHAPTER 1

THE SPIRIT OF DISTRACTION

"But Martha was distracted with much serving, and she approached Him and said,

'Lord, do You not care that my sister has left me to serve alone?

Therefore tell her to help me.' And Jesus answered and said to her,

'Martha, Martha, you are worried and troubled about many things. But one thing is needed, and Mary has chosen that good part, which will not be taken away from her.'"
—Luke 10:40-42, NKJV

Do you know someone who is always busy for the Lord? We call that type of person a "Martha," and they are a necessary part of the Kingdom. We can't ignore their importance or negate their contributions. We love and appreciate their selfless service, dependability, and willingness to show up and be counted among the workers for Christ.

Sometimes, like Martha, we get so busy that we lose track of the most important thing in life—our relationship with our Heavenly Father. When that happens, we can fall victim to the spirit of distraction. When the spirit of distraction gets hold of us, it keeps us from fulfilling our purpose, causes us to get sidetracked, veer off course, stumble, lose our focus, and derail our God-given destiny. Letting the spirit of distraction get a foothold in your life can be fatal to your faith.

To distract means to draw or lead attention in different directions at the same time. It's a way to stir up or confuse our emotions and motives, and the Word of God contains many examples of the spirit of distraction. Satan wants to abort God's plan for your life, so he will attempt to distract you using a series of roadblocks and detours to keep you from your destiny. He will try to break your focus and cause hindrances to keep you from fulfilling your purpose for the Kingdom.

In Scripture, we read how God gave Abraham a promise that He would bless him with a son in his old age. But Abraham became impatient, as many of us do today, and he grew weary of waiting. So he took matters into his own hands.

"And Sarai, Abram's wife, took Hagar her maid the Egyptian, after Abram had dwelt ten years in the land of Canaan, and gave her to her husband Abram to be his wife. And he went in unto Hagar, and she conceived: and when she saw that she had conceived, her mistress was despised in her eyes." (Genesis 16:3-4).

Abraham got distracted. Instead of waiting for God, he accepted Sarah's offer and took her maid as his wife to have a child with her. Two wives under one roof didn't work out, and eventually, Hagar and her son had to leave. Years later, when Isaac was a boy, and Abraham took him to Mount Moriah to sacrifice him during God's test (Genesis 22:1-19), Scripture mentions three times that Isaac was Abraham's son—his *only* son. God's plan for his people didn't involve Ishmael, who was the result of Abraham's distraction.

Samson, the strongest man in the world when the Spirit of the Lord came upon him, (Judges 15:14) allowed a woman named Delilah to distract him when the Lords of the Philistines paid her 1,100 silver coins to find out the secret of his great strength. The Bible says she pressured him every day until he was so annoyed that he revealed the secret—his long hair. After a visit from the Philistine barbers, God's strength departed from him, his eyes were put out, and he spent the rest of his life in slavery.

King Solomon, considered the richest man that ever lived, was distracted by the luxuries of life and women. King Solomon had seven hundred wives and three hundred concubines (I Kings 11:3) comprised of foreign princesses including Moabites, Sidonites, Hittites, Ammonites, and even Pharaoh's daughter.

We can only imagine the incredible distraction he lived under with a thousand women at his disposal. Which makes one think: if it's hard for a guy to listen to one woman, can you imagine trying to listen to a thousand? Marriage counseling anyone?

But seriously, even today it's easy to get distracted by the opposite sex, causing us to lose our focus on God.

As the nation of Israel approached the Promised Land, Moses sent twelve men to spy it out. (Number 13:1-33). When they returned, ten men gave a negative report; only Joshua and Caleb came back with a positive one. Each of the twelve had seen the inhabitants of the land, calling them "giants," but they didn't all see the challenge the same way. While the ten focused on the size of the enemy, Joshua and

Caleb focused on the size of their God and didn't allow the other spies to distract them. Ten were distracted, and it caused them to miss out on God's plan and purpose. Joshua and Caleb stayed focused, and they were permitted to cross into the Promised Land. These two men of faith didn't tell God how big the giants were; they told the people how big God was. The Father kept Joshua and Caleb young and healthy and rewarded them for their faith and reliance on Him.

"But without faith, it is impossible to please him: for he that cometh to God must believe that he is, and that he is a rewarder of them that diligently seek him." (Hebrews 11:6).

Scripture is loaded with examples of great men and women of God who didn't allow distractions to keep them from their appointed tasks (check out some of their stories in the Book of Hebrews, Chapter 11, a portion of the Bible often referred to as "The Hall of Faith").

The enemy will use anything or anyone to distract you. Even modern technology has proven to involve the spirit of distraction.

When cell phones and texting became popular, it was a very exciting time. But it's become a destructive distraction, as many have lost their lives due to texting while driving. Social media, television, video games, and many other technological advances have become time-wasters, distracting God's people from living to their fullest potential. And as technology continues to advance, the spirit of distraction is advancing as well. We have become like children on Christmas morning. Now tell me; if we can't even focus on a single toy, how can we focus on God's plans for our lives?

The spirit of distraction has succeeded in destroying the God-given destiny of far too many Christians.

One of the most potent, yet discreet, weapons used by the Devil is the power of distraction, using it to confuse our thinking and prevent us from praying and studying God's Word.

Delays and detours are all distractions to your destiny, which is why we are instructed in Scripture to take every thought captive. (II Corinthians 10:5).

CHAPTER 2

THE SPIRIT OF FEAR

"I sought the LORD, and he heard me,
and delivered me from all my fears."
—Psalm 34:4

What if I were to ask you about the things you are fearful about? How would you answer the question? You might answer with a long list of phobias, or you might puff out your chest and say, "Nothing! I'm fearless!" In my research on the subject, I discovered that there are over 500 phobias, ranging from arachnophobia (the fear of spiders) to Philophobia (the fear of falling in love). Certain types of fear are simply part of the human condition, and as long as we're in these earthly bodies, we'll have times when fear creeps into our thoughts. When it does, we must be on our guard to make sure it doesn't take up permanent residence in our lives, and we need to discern the source of the fear.

Fear can be used by the Devil as he tries to hinder us in our relationship with God. Fear can create a condition known as analysis paralysis—causing us to avoid making a proper decision or taking action on important issues. Satan knows that fear has this type of effect, and he will use it against the saints to keep us from our destinies in Christ.

Chronic fear can have long-term effects on our bodies, our brains, and our outlook on life. It creates anxiety, which creates stress, which changes the way we see the world. It can also impact physiological functioning of our bodies, change our brain chemistry, affect digestion, raise blood pressure, interfere with sleep, give place for diseases to get a foothold, and create anger or helplessness. The longer we live in a spirit of fear, the more negative things we will see birthed and grown in our lives, and the more unproductive we will become in the Kingdom of God.

Scripture makes it quite clear that the spirit of fear is from Satan. "For God has not given us a spirit of fear, but of power and of love and of a sound mind." (2 Timothy 1:7).

The enemy's plans are no surprise to our God, and that's why the Bible contains God's instructions about fear more than 100 times: be not afraid, fear not, do not fear, do not be afraid. God knew that we would encounter situations of uncertainty and would react with fear, so He told us ahead of time how to handle it.

"The Lord is my light and my salvation; whom shall I fear? The Lord is the strength of my life; of whom shall I be afraid?" (Psalm 27:1).

Fear is a basic instinct that instantaneously causes changes in the amygdala of the brain, creating a desire to either fight or run. God created us with this primal response to warn us of danger so we would be careful when standing at the edge of a cliff, encountering a poisonous snake that could bite us, getting too close to fire, or any number of physical dangers that require swift reaction to avoid harm. In its created form, this God-given instinct is a wonderful gift designed to protect us from harm.

But Satan isn't referred to as an "angel of light" for nothing (II Corinthians 11:14). He can and will twist the good things of God into negative things that will affect our lives in adverse ways. For some, he has turned fear into the go-to reaction that keeps them from God's best. And when the spirit of fear gets a stronghold, we tend to focus more on the problem instead of focusing on the One who can solve it. Fear is the lie that makes us cry; makes us feel helpless and hopeless; and leaves us disheartened and discouraged.

"For I the Lord thy God will hold thy right hand, saying unto thee, fear not; I will help thee." (Isaiah 41:13).

The spirit of fear is a deadly weapon that can cause as much devastation to God's people as a nuclear bomb causes in the physical world. If we allow the spirit of fear to grip our hearts, it will freeze our ability to be objective. Look around, and you'll see many people gripped in fear that keeps them from doing what would make them happy or what God is calling them to do.

Consider the widow whose husband was abusive before he died. Her fear of giving her love to another man has caused her to be single for over twenty-five years. Living alone for over two decades, she has decided that a lonely lifestyle is easier to live with than another abusive relationship. The spirit of fear has seized her heart and mind, and she refuses to give any man a chance.

On the other hand, there are women that stay in abusive relationships because the spirit of fear whispers to them that it's better to be abused than to be alone. They won't try to end the abuse either; fearing retaliation if they leave or worse yet—in their minds—the abuser leaving. They fail to realize that they are being held in bondage by a spirit of fear, and if they would simply turn to God, He will protect them from their abusers and deliver them from all of their fears.

"The fear of man bringeth a snare: but whoso putteth his trust in the Lord shall be safe." (Proverbs 29:25).

The spirit of fear can weaken our faith; leading to habits that destroy our peace, cloud our judgment, and impact our families. Many of the common ailments in America today are rooted in the spirit of fear, such as alcoholism, drug abuse, and sexual immorality.

When I'm working with people dealing with fear, I often ask these questions:

- What would you be doing if you weren't afraid?
- Where would you go?
- What would you say and to whom would you say it?
- What would you do differently than you're doing now?

How would you answer these questions about your life? You'd probably get a pretty good indication of where the fear has built a stronghold in your walk with God. But you most likely already know the areas where fear has been holding your happiness hostage; you just may not know how to overcome it.

> "And he said unto his disciples, 'Therefore I say unto you. Take not thought for your life, what ye shall eat; neither for the body, what ye shall put on. The life is more than meat, and the body is more than raiment. Consider the ravens: for they neither sow nor reap; which neither have storehouse nor barn; and God feedeth them; how much more are ye better than the fowls? And which of you with taking thought can

> add to his stature one cubit? If ye then be not able to that thing which is least, why take ye thought for the rest? (Luke 12:22-26)

God's Word also says, "Be careful for nothing; but in every thing by prayer and supplication with thanksgiving let your requests be made known unto God. And the peace of God, which passeth all understanding, shall keep your hearts and minds through Christ Jesus." (Philippians 4:6-7).

The opposite of fear can be described as walking in assurance, being bold (without being conceited), and possessing an air of confidence and courage. So one of the secrets to casting out the spirit of fear from our lives is to take our place in Christ while taking hold of the opposite.

If we let him, God will turn our doubt into assurance (Psalm 23:4), our worry into boldness (Hebrews 4:16), our negative thoughts and expectations into confidence (Proverbs 3:26), and our fear into courage (Deuteronomy 31:6).

We have been letting the Devil steal our joy by using the spirit of fear for far too long. We need to bring an end to the torment of this joy-robbing spirit. It's time to bind it, not live behind it. It's time to cast it out, instead of trying to last it out. It's time to live in peace instead of pieces as we reclaim our lives, our loves, and our dreams.

"There is no fear in love; but perfect love casteth out fear: because fear hath torment. He that feareth is not made perfect in love. (1 John 4:18).

CHAPTER 3

THE SPIRIT OF SAUL

"For where envying and strife is,
there is confusion and every evil work."
—James 3:16

Young David, a man after God's own heart (Acts 13:22), was placed in the hands of King Saul; a selfish, jealous, and insecure person. Saul was extremely jealous of David because God had chosen him to be king when Saul's reign was over. His selfish, threatening leadership made it obvious that he had no intention of making room for David as his successor. In Saul's eyes, David was a threat to his monarchy.

It's hard to be a David in a Saul's house, but the Bible says that David behaved himself wisely before Saul.

> "Wherefore Saul sent messengers unto Jesse, and said, 'send me David thy son, which is with the sheep.' And Jesse took an ass laden with bread, and a bottle of wine, and a kid, and sent them by David his son unto Saul. And David came to Saul, and stood before him: and he loved him greatly; and he became his armor bearer. And Saul sent to Jesse, saying, 'Let David, I

> pray thee, stand before me; for he hath found favour in my sight.'
>
> "And it came to pass, when the evil spirit from God was upon Saul, that David took an harp, and played with his hand: so Saul was refreshed, and was well, and the evil spirit departed from him." (I Samuel 16:19-23).

Although David would have been justified to harm King Saul for the evil treatment he received, he chose to not kill the king when he had the chance.

"And David said to Abishai, 'Destroy him not: for who can stretch forth his hand against the Lord's anointed, and be guiltless?' David said furthermore, 'As the Lord liveth, the Lord shall smite him; or his day shall come to die; or he shall descend into battle, and perish.'" (I Samuel 26:9-10).

David chose not to seek revenge and kill King Saul. Although he had plenty of opportunities, David refused to touch God's anointed. In the end, King Saul killed himself, and David's hands remained clean.

We can learn a lot from the story of Saul and David because the spirit that worked in Saul's life is still at work in many of today's leaders. Motivated by jealousy, they lead using intimidation and manipulation. Those who operate under the spirit of jealousy, which I call the spirit of Saul, hate to see others succeed or advance. When someone with the spirit of Saul has authority over us, it's difficult to work, worship, witness, or win. They will plan, ploy, and plot against our success. They will set traps, tell lies, falsely accuse, rationalize, threaten, and do whatever is necessary to hold us down or knock us out of the game.

Some of us have to fight the spirit of Saul every day at home, with our coworkers, or in our ministries. But it probably doesn't have anything to do with us directly. More than likely, it's the jealous spirit of Saul working against us. When dealing with someone who has the spirit of Saul, we shouldn't expect to get help, support, or encouragement from those who lead us.

When the spirit of Saul confronts us, we must ask God for wisdom on how to deal with it before we take action. While we need to equip ourselves to deal with it, it's important to remember that God sometimes puts this spirit in our path to teach us something. We need to take the high road like David did and let God fight the battle for us.

"Dearly beloved, avenge not yourselves, but rather give place unto wrath: for it is written, 'Vengeance is mine; I will repay,' saith the Lord." (Romans 12:19).

The spirit of Saul is found many times in the book of Genesis. Cain killed Abel because of jealousy. Joseph's brothers sold him into slavery because they were jealous that he was his father's favorite son. Laban cheated and tricked Jacob multiple times because of jealousy.

Laban's treatment of Jacob demonstrates an important point about the spirit of Saul as it is often a direct consequence of insecurity. Laban lived with the fear that Jacob would eventually be more prosperous than he, even fearing that Jacob would take his wives and children away. But God appeared to Laban in a dream and told him not to do anything to Jacob, good or bad. God fought the spirit of Saul for Jacob, and in the end, Laban entered into a covenant with Jacob: "This heap be witness, and this pillar be witness, that I will not pass over this heap to thee, and that thou shalt not pass over this heap and this pillar unto me, for harm." (Genesis 31: 52).

As a minister of the Gospel, I've heard stories about how jealous and insecure saints have fought to exclude new members from the church and new coworkers from their place of employment. Are you someone living under the influence of the spirit of Saul? Think about these questions:

- Do you hate to see others succeed in the Kingdom of God?
- Do you resent watching others grow in faith?
- Do you intentionally fail to honor or praise your brothers and sisters in Christ?
- Do you hate to hear another person getting praised?
- Does it irritate you when someone else gets promoted?
- Do you get angry when someone speaks well of someone you don't like?

If you answered yes to even one of the questions above, you need God to remove the spirit of Saul from your life.

When a person is suspected of having heart disease, a cardiologist will run a test commonly referred to as an EKG or ECG (electrocardiogram). Many of God's people are suffering from a type spiritual heart disease. We need to ask the Holy Spirit to give us a spiritual electrocardiogram every day, and then allow Dr. Jesus to heal our jealous hearts.

"Create in me a clean heart, O God; and renew a right spirit within me." (Psalm 51:10).

Growing up in ministry from a very young age, I tried to serve God with a pure heart. I had no hidden agendas; I just felt it was a privilege to serve. Even though I was well-liked and respected among my peers, I personally experienced one negative encounter after another. It turned out that not everyone was as happy about my success as I was.

The spirit of Saul will cause jealousy to rise up in other people and come against us, so it's important to prepare our hearts for the opposition that will result. Success breeds jealousy, whether you're in business or ministry. And as God's favor brings us success, it's important to get a spiritual EKG every day to make sure we don't fall to this jealous spirit. People with the spirit of Saul love success; they just hate successful people.

"Now the works of the flesh are evident: sexual immorality, impurity, sensuality, idolatry, sorcery, enmity, strife, **jealousy**, fits of anger, rivalries, dissensions, divisions, envy, drunkenness, orgies, and things like these. I warn you, as I warned you before, that those who do such things will not inherit the kingdom of God." (Galatians 5:19-21, ESV, emphasis by the author).

CHAPTER 4

THE SPIRIT OF GOSSIP

"Death and life are in the power of the tongue: and they that love it shall eat the fruit thereof."
—Proverbs 18:21

British musician and former member of the Beatles, George Harrison, once called gossip the Devil's radio. Small talk isn't always small, and chit chat or hearsay isn't harmless because it is almost always at the expense of another. Gossip is bad news, never glad news. And if we were to be completely honest with ourselves, we are drawn to it like flies to a cow patty.

"The words of a whisperer are like dainty morsels, and they go down into the innermost parts of the body." (Proverbs 18:8 NASB).

Gossip is "mmm, mmm good." We chow down on those sweet, juicy morsels as if we were eating our favorite dessert. And sometimes, it's so sweet and so juicy, that we share our dessert with others to enjoy (Proverbs 20:19). Before you know it, everyone has an upset stomach.

Was there ever a time in your life when someone started vicious rumors about you? It hurt, didn't it? The old adage that "s may break your bones, but words can never hurt you" is simply not true. Gossip kills! It kills our witness! It kills our relationship with God! It kills our relationships with our brothers and sisters in the Body of Christ! It kills reputations! It kills careers! It kills marriages! It kills friendships! It kills churches!

An unknown author wrote a poem that sums up gossip very succinctly:

MY NAME IS GOSSIP

(Author Unknown)

My name is Gossip.
I have no respect for justice.
I maim without killing.
I break hearts and ruin lives.
I am cunning and malicious and
gather strength with age.
The more I am quoted the more I am believed.
I flourish at every level of society.
My victims are helpless.
They cannot protect themselves against me
because I have no name and no face.
To track me down is impossible.
The harder you try, the more elusive I become.
I am nobody's friend.
Once I tarnish a reputation, it is never the same.
I topple governments and ruin marriages.
I ruin careers and cause sleepless nights,
heartache and indigestion.
I spawn suspicion and generate grief.
I make innocent people cry in their pillows.
Even my name hisses.
I am called Gossip.

As mature Christians, we should know better than to run around talking about other people and telling secrets. We should refuse to participate in this destructive practice by keeping our ears and mouths shut to gossip.

"A talebearer revealeth secrets: but he that is of a faithful spirit concealeth the matter." (Proverbs 11:13).

"Death and life are in the power of the tongue: and they that love it shall eat the fruit thereof." (Proverbs 18:21).

I hope you see just how destructive the spirit of gossip can be. When we allow things to fly off our tongues before we ever give thought to what we're saying or the consequences our words will have, we not only damage the person we are gossiping about, we are also damaging our own reputations because we become known as talebearers and lose the respect of our peers. We need to stop to think about what we're saying when we speak about others. The spirit of gossip depends on big mouths and eager ears.

"Wrongdoers eagerly listen to gossip; liars pay close attention to slander." (Proverbs 17:4 New Living Translation).

"The one who guards his mouth preserves his life; the one who opens wide his lips comes to ruin." (Proverbs 13:3).

If we develop the reputation of being a gossip, most people will choose not to associate with us. They know that if we talk about other people, we'll likely talk about them too.

"Finally, brethren, whatsoever things are true, whatsoever things are honest, whatsoever things are just, whatsoever things are pure, whatsoever things are lovely, whatsoever things are of good report; if there be any virtue and if there be any praise, think on these things." (Philippians 4:8).

When a Christian refuses to listen to or spread gossip, it will stop. Proverbs 26:20 assures us, "Where no wood is, there the fire goeth out: so where there is no talebearer, the strife ceaseth."

Scripture is plain about gossip and lies, which is why we must always be careful with the words we speak. Matthew 12:36-37 warns us, "But I say unto you, that every idle word that men shall speak, they shall give account thereof in the day of judgment. For by thy words thou shalt be justified, and by thy words thou shalt be condemned."

To shut down the spirit of gossip and its roots, go to the source. The enemy will always flee when his lies are brought into the light of the truth. If the church leadership is entertaining gossip, take it to the pastor. As a pastor, I know that we must always deal with the spirit of gossip decisively and quickly. Ephesians 5:11 tells us not to initially expose unfruitful works of darkness, but instead to talk privately with the person involved. If all else fails, we are to have no fellowship with those involved in unfruitful works.

"Moreover, if thy brother shall trespass against thee, go and tell him his fault between thee and him alone: if he shall hear thee, thou hast gained thy brother. But if he will not hear thee, then take with thee one or two more, that in the mouth of two or three witnesses every word may be established. And if he shall neglect to hear them, tell it unto the church: but if he neglects to hear the church, let him be unto thee as an heathen man and a publican." (Matthew 18:15-17).

Every church would be wise to make it clear that the spirit of gossip will not be tolerated for any reason. Church leadership should never entertain someone who wants to gossip about another in church or about the people in leadership. Those with the spirit of gossip lose all credibility with the people they minister to because they demonstrate traits and behaviors that don't line up with Scripture.

We need to stop allowing the spirit of gossip to operate in our lives, and that includes gossip in the form of a prayer request too.

"Set a watch, O Lord, before my mouth; keep the door of my lips." (Psalm 141:3).

CHAPTER 5

THE SPIRIT OF PRIDE

"Pride goeth before destruction,
and an haughty spirit before a fall."
—Proverbs 16:18

In my book, *Leadership from Behind the Scenes*,[2] I addressed pride as a deadly spirit that is almost invisible to the person who is controlled by it, but visible to everyone who comes in contact with it. It's colorless, odorless, and definitely tasteless (in all connotations of the word). I equated it (and still do) to bad breath—everyone can smell it except the person who has it.

The spirit of pride can cause us to engage in stinkin' thinkin'. We end up thinking more of ourselves than others do which makes it hard to be taught because we think we're above our leaders and teachers. When the spirit of pride controls us, we are seldom happy. We are rarely satisfied as we continually seek the affirmation of others to match our inflated self-image, and we get upset when others don't provide it.

---

2 Dr. Ron Webb, Leadership From Behind the Scenes (Chalfant Eckert Publishing, Rolla, MO, ©2015) page 32

"For all that is in the world, the lust of the flesh, and the lust of the eyes, and the pride of life, is not of the Father, but is of the world." (I John 2:16).

Pride has led to the downfall of angels and men. In heaven, Lucifer's pride led to rebellion when he and a third of the angels turned against God, causing Lucifer to be cast out. Can you imagine being in God's presence daily and getting thrown out of heaven because of the haughty spirit of pride?

"Every one that is proud in heart is an abomination to the Lord: though hand join in hand, he shall not be unpunished." (Proverbs 16:5).

God opposes the proud and gives grace to the humble. (James 4:6). When people look at a Christian, they're supposed to see Jesus. Not a single moment of our Savior's life on this earth was spent in pride.

> "Let this mind be in you, which was also in Christ Jesus: Who, being in the form of God, thought it not robbery to be equal with God: But made himself of no reputation, and took upon him the form of a servant, and was made in the likeness of men: And being found in fashion as a man, he humbled himself, and became obedient unto death, even the death of the cross.
>
> "Wherefore God also hath highly exalted him, and given him a name which is above every name: That at the name of Jesus every knee should bow, of things in heaven, and things in earth, and things under the earth; and that every tongue should confess that Jesus Christ is Lord, to the glory of God the Father." (Philippians 2:5-11).

He was born in a lowly manger. (Luke 2:1-20). When he came into his ministry, he spoke with authority (Matthew 7:29) but did not boast of anything but His Father in heaven. He let God do the boasting for him.

Just as it was with Jesus, if we will humble ourselves before God, He will lift us up. (James 4:10). When we exalt ourselves, we take credit for the things God has done for us and given us.

The spirit of pride may cause us to boast of riches, but it is God who makes us rich, and it is God who gives us the ability to get wealth.

"The blessing of the LORD, it maketh rich, and he addeth no sorrow with it." (Proverbs 10:22).

Danger exists for those who trust in riches because such trust is evidence of the spirit of pride. Proverbs 11:28 tells us that those who trust in riches will fall. The spirit of pride leads to bragging about the things we accumulate, and that causes us to feel that we're better than everyone else. Scripture is clear about earthly riches and their true value:

"Do not store up for yourselves treasures on earth, where moths and vermin destroy, and where thieves break in and steal" (Matthew 6:19, NIV).

God owns the cattle on a thousand hills and has so much gold that He paves the streets of heaven with it. If we put our possessions above God's provision, we are guilty of an abomination to Almighty God.

The spirit of pride is one of the primary causes of divorce; in the world and in the church. When counseling troubled marriages, pastors often hear the spirit of pride as couples attempt to rationalize their actions:

1. Nothing's ever his fault.
2. I feel manipulated.

3. She's never wrong.
4. He says he forgives but then keeps bringing it up.
5. He acts like he's God.
6. She makes me feel inferior and small like I'm not good enough.
7. Being married to her isn't fun; it's a constant struggle.

Does any of that sound familiar? We need to cast out the spirit of pride if it does. Getting pride under control can save our homes.

"Only by pride cometh contention: but with the well advised is wisdom." (Proverbs 13:10).

Joseph Benson in his commentaries on the Old Testament[3] explained that pride makes a man self-conceited in his opinions, obstinate in his resolutions, and impatient of any opposition. Is it any wonder God opposes the spirit of pride?

"These six things doth the Lord hate: yea, seven are an abomination unto him: **A proud look**, a lying tongue, and hands that shed innocent blood, An heart that deviseth wicked imaginations, feet that be swift in running to mischief, a false witness that speaketh lies, and he that soweth discord among brethren." (Proverbs 6:16-19, emphasis by author).

One of the primary reasons the Pharisees were failing God's people was the spirit of pride. They were arrogant about everything, including fasting. In one of his confrontations with the Pharisees, Jesus told a parable that explained heaven's position of pride.

---

3 Joseph Benson, Commentary on the Old and New Testament, 5 volumes, 1811-1826, in public domain

> "And he spake this parable unto certain which trusted in themselves that they were righteous, and despised others: two men went up into the temple to pray; the one a Pharisee, and the other a publican.
>
> "The Pharisee stood and prayed thus with himself, God, I thank thee, that I am not as other men are, extortioners, unjust, adulterers, or even as this publican. I fast twice in the week, I give tithes of all that I possess.
>
> "And the publican, standing afar off, would not lift up so much as his eyes unto heaven, but smote upon his breast, saying, 'God be merciful to me a sinner.'
>
> "I tell you, this man went down to his house justified rather than the other: or every one that exalteth himself shall be abased; and he that humbleth himself shall be exalted." (Luke 18:9-14).

God is so serious about keeping pride out of our lives that He warned Timothy not to put an inexperienced person in a position of ministerial authority because the spirit of pride may creep in:

"Not a novice, lest being lifted up with pride he fall into the condemnation of the devil." (1 Timothy 3:6).

Pride is a sin, and many call it a root sin because other sins come from it. Prideful people hold grudges, refuse to forgive, and won't listen to others who disagree with them. They are unwilling to submit to the authority of leaders appointed over them, frequently gossip, are judgmental, are easily offended, and are opinionated. Their attitudes and behaviors interfere with the functioning of the Body of Christ. Like a diseased liver or cancerous colon, the whole body suffers because one part malfunctions and needs treatment.

HOW DO WE GET RID OF THE SPIRIT OF PRIDE?

We have to come to God in prayer, and expose it to the light of the Scripture. If possible, we should find an accountability partner to help us recognize it (along with any of the other spirits we discuss in this book), along with its foul smell. We need to focus on the virtues that oppose pride and cultivate them instead: humility, compassion, and forgiveness. It might also be necessary to ask forgiveness from those we have offended or harmed by our pride.

Above all, we need to ask God to forgive us and to help us develop better ways of interacting with people. When the spirit of pride controls us, we are demonstrating our insecurity in our relationship with God. Only by His forgiveness can we conquer the spirit of pride.

CHAPTER 6

THE SPIRIT OF LEVIATHAN

"That day the Lord with his sore and great and strong sword shall punish leviathan the piercing serpent, even leviathan that crooked serpent; and he shall slay the dragon that is in the sea."
—Isaiah 27:1

You may not be familiar with the spirit of Leviathan. I must admit, it was unknown to me; although I had seen it in operation, I just didn't have a name for it. The spirit of Leviathan is king over all the children of pride. (Job 41:32). Scripture represents it in several ways, including a crocodile and a sea serpent, and it literally means "twisted" or "coiled." Leviathan often brings significant attacks against leadership, and it causes people to act arrogant, puffed up, and envious. This is a deadly spirit—like the spirit of pride on steroids.

To understand the destructive power of the spirit of Leviathan, we need to look no further than the Garden of Eden. The serpent was subtler and craftier than any living creature and tricked Eve by twisting God's words, so she was willing to eat of the tree of knowledge of good and evil (Genesis 3:1).

"But of the fruit of the tree which is in the midst of the garden, God hath said, 'Ye shall not eat of it, neither shall ye touch it, lest ye die.' And the serpent said unto the woman, 'Ye shall not surely die: For God doth know that in the day ye eat thereof, then your eyes shall be opened, and ye shall be as gods, knowing good and evil.'" (Genesis 3:3-5).

And mankind has been falling under the influence of the spirit of Leviathan ever since.

Leviathan jams up our line of communication with God by using harsh words spoken softly, and it's very dangerous to the saints who possess the Holy Spirit. When the wires of communication get all twisted up, we can experience a short circuit in the communion between our spirit and the Spirit of God. When that happens, we get confused, which is exactly what Satan wants, because confusion hinders God's work. "For God is not the author of confusion, but of peace, as in all churches of the saints." (1 Corinthians 14:33).

When we find ourselves in a state of confusion, we can rest assured that the spirit of Leviathan is at work. This is why we must guard our hearts and minds against this spirit at all times.

"Beloved, do not believe every spirit, but test the spirits, whether they are of God; because many false prophets have gone out into the world." (1 John 4:1).

When the spirit of Leviathan plagues us, we might be tempted to reject efforts to be delivered from its hold on our lives. I know this might sound weird, but sometimes we choose to hold on to the things holding us down because we think it's better to hide our past instead of deal with it. As the children of Adam, we are born with a sinful nature that can be pretty hard to let go of. We accept the lie that a little sin for a season doesn't really hurt anyone, so let's have a little fun.

The spirit of Leviathan is also a covenant-breaking spirit. Paul told Timothy that in the last days there would be lots of covenants broken (II Timothy 3:3). Brothers and sisters who used to work hand-in-hand and side-by-side are now adversaries because somewhere along the way, they broke their covenant with each other.

The spirit of Leviathan also breeds selfishness, causing believers to abandon the gifts of hospitality and service. When this happens, an attitude of "my way or the highway" can develop, destroying the building up of the body. It can create stubbornness and hardheartedness, an unforgiving attitude, and a person totally void of compassion.

The spirit of Leviathan can actually cause physical discomfort, such as a feeling of being smothered or having difficulty breathing. In the Bible, breath and wind have to do with the Holy Spirit, so when Leviathan tries to smother out the Holy Spirit, causing you to break fellowship and covenant with God, it can have a physical effect.

"His scales are his pride, shut up together as with a close seal. One is so near to another that no air can come between them." (Job 41:15-16).

Have you ever witnessed symptoms of the spirit of Leviathan in your church? Many scholars have debated, but most agree with these symptoms and methods of attack.

SYMPTOMS

1. Superior attitudes toward others in the church
2. A self-governing attitude
3. Taking glory for things God has done
4. Having confidence in oneself above those in authority over us

5. Looking down on others in the church as being lesser Christians
6. Lack of actually spending quality time with God
7. Judgmental and accusing thoughts and attitudes
8. Bragging over revelations and achievements
9. Discrediting those in authority
10. Desirous of being served
11. Striving for a high reputation
12. Quick to control others
13. Using position of authority or God-given gifts to satisfy self-centered ambition and vision
14. Disrespectful, mocking, or speaking against deliverance and deliverance ministries

METHOD OF ATTACK

1. Lying, gossiping, accusations, criticizing and finding fault with others, slandering
2. Miscommunication
3. Prophetic word will be attacked
4. Temptations of pride
5. Putting trust in things other than intimacy with God

The spirit of Leviathan can be overcome through the power of the Holy Spirit. When we recognize the influence of Leviathan, we must repent quickly and allow the Holy Spirit to work in the hearts of those who've caused the injury. We also must be willing to submit to others as stated in I Peter 5:5. "Likewise, ye younger, submit yourselves unto the elder. Yea, all of you be subject one to another, and be clothed with humility: for God resisteth the proud, and giveth grace to the humble."

As leaders, we must always guard our hearts against the influence of pride. One way to do this is by making the conscious decision to walk humbly with our God. Humility doesn't mean we walk around with our heads hanging down and acting timidly. True humility is walking with the knowledge that we need God, that we can do nothing without Him, and that it is only by His grace and mercy that we can can fulfill His call on our lives.

CHAPTER 7

THE SPIRIT OF ABSALOM

"Whosoever therefore resisteth the power, resisteth the ordinance of God: and they that resist shall receive to themselves damnation."
—Romans 13:2

David's son Amnon had an unhealthy crush on his step-sister Tamar, but he thought what he was feeling was love. And to validate his unhealthy feelings, Amnon faked being sick to get Tamar to his bedside. In his lust he raped her, and then he threw her out of his bedchamber like he would a prostitute. In the end, he hated her with more intensity than he had previously lusted for her.

David's other son, Absalom, wanted vengeance against Amnon for what he'd done to Tamar, but he kept his anger and bitterness in check as he waited for the right time to exact his revenge. After two years had passed, Absalom had his opportunity. He partied with Amnon, and after getting him drunk, Absalom had his servants kill Amnon to avenge Tamar's rape. Knowing that he must find a way to tell his father about Amnon's death, Absalom developed a cunning lie.

Did you ever hear the story about the boy who got an "F" on his report card? To soften the news to his dad, he told him about eloping with the girl next door because she was pregnant. At the end of his letter, he tells his dad that none of it was true, but that he should remember that there are worse things he could do than get a bad grade on his report card. Absalom did something like that.

He sent word to his father David, that he had killed all the sons of David, and that everyone was dead except Absalom. Then while King David was grieving, Absalom told him that the message was incorrect. Only Amnon was dead, so things weren't as bad as they originally had seemed.

Absalom fled from his home and was gone for three years when David began to miss him. The worst of David's grieving was over, so he brought Absalom back into the fold and forgave him. That turned out to be a bad move. Absalom was still the same conniving person he had always been. And he continued to carry bitterness and rebellion in his heart—a condition the Bible likens to witchcraft.

"For rebellion is as the sin of witchcraft, and stubbornness is as iniquity and idolatry." (I Samuel, 15:23).

Absalom wanted his father's kingdom. He would smile to his father's face while figuratively stabbing him in the back. Absalom would send out mounted guards before him every day as a show of his kingly behavior, and he sat in the gateway of the city talking with the people to seek out those with grievances and complaints against David. Playing the role of politician, he promised to settle matters for them if they would help him become king. He showed them kindness and made them feel important, not because he meant it, but because he was sly and had the ulterior motive of damaging his father's leadership. Absalom won the hearts of the people using charm, cunning, trickery, deceit, and taking kernels of truth to build grandiose lies to win the favor of the people.

Over time, Absalom undermined his father's authority, and damaged David's favor with the people behind the scenes. Eventually, Absalom's scheme fell apart, he fell from favor, and died a painful death. (II Samuel 13-19).

What does this story have to do with today's church? It serves as a warning for us to guard our ministries against the spirit of Absalom. People under the control of this spirit are on a path of destruction and will work to intentionally cause division and strife in the church. And while doing so, they will be charming, cunning, and slick about getting what they want.

The spirit of Absalom uses people who are malcontented or disgruntled. It intentionally looks for people who are hurting, especially if they feel wounded by the church. This spirit's charm is to act as a balm to spiritual wounds, but with a salve of ulterior motives. People with the spirit of Absalom are like false prophets who come as ravenous wolves in sheep's clothing. (Matthew 7:15).

"Now I beseech you, brethren, mark them which cause divisions and offences contrary to the doctrine which ye have learned; and avoid them. For they that are such serve not our Lord Jesus Christ, but their own belly; and by good words and fair speeches deceive the hearts of the simple." (Romans 16:17-18).

People with the spirit of Absalom are especially hard to deal with because they have gained the favor of many in the church and have their own following or clique. They have power because their charms are hard to resist. Unfortunately, their rebellion is subtle and hard to identify until the damage is already done.

Here are some signs that the spirit of Absalom is operating in your church:

1. Gossiping about others in the church.
2. Disloyalty, murmurings, and faultfinding about church leadership that take place outside the earshot of the leaders being criticized. People with the spirit of Absalom sow seeds of discontent and make people believe that authority is incompetent or not trustworthy.
3. Members who stop interacting with the Body of Christ, who ban together and do little to edify and fortify the church.
4. Church members who want to separate and start their own churches. This can include conspiracy that turns into open rebellion. Churches planted as the outcome of the spirit of Absalom will not survive or succeed.
5. Argumentative members who are against everything the church leaders try to do. They have their own visions and have to be right, so the leadership must be wrong. They appear to be in competition with church leadership.
6. Members who are easily offended and bitter.
7. Spiritual pride and independence from spiritual authority.

The spirit of Absalom can completely destroy a church and its people. People under the influence of this spirit sound Scriptural, even spiritual. But it brings nothing but death.

In my book, *Leadership from Behind the Scenes*,[4] I shared how the only way to deal with the spirit of Absalom is to cut off all ties to it. Often, people with this spirit leave the church out of rebellion but want to stay in fellowship with those in the church. It may sound harmless, even good, but their motives are not for fellowship, they are for division. It's our job as church leaders to confront the spirit and speak the truth in love. Pastors must shepherd the flock, and protect the sheep from the wolves.

"This know also, that in the last days perilous times shall come. For men shall be lovers of their own selves, covetous, boasters, proud, blasphemers, disobedient to parents, unthankful, unholy, without natural affection, trucebreakers, false accusers, incontinent, fierce, despisers of those that are good, traitors, heady, highminded, lovers of pleasures more than lovers of God; having a form of godliness, but denying the power thereof: from such turn away." (2 Timothy 3:1-5).

4 Ibid, page 53

CHAPTER 8

THE SPIRIT OF SEDUCTION

"Now the Spirit speaketh expressly, that in the latter times some shall depart from the faith, giving heed to seducing spirits, and doctrines of devils."
—1 Timothy 4:1

When we think of seducing spirits, we quickly think of sexual persuasion. That may be an accurate assumption most of the time, but it's not the only way the spirit of seduction entices people. Webster's dictionary defines the word *seduce* as:

1. To attract or lead (someone) away from proper behavior or thinking
2. To induce (someone) to engage in sexual activity, as by flirting or persuasion
3. To entice into a different state or position

When we see the word in the Bible, it is used to describe the man who is being led away from the path of truth, causing him to abandon his faith. A picture of such deceit can be found in the story of how the serpent seduced Adam and Eve (Genesis 3). Strong's Concordance shows the word has several meanings which equate to being deceived or hoodwinked. It describes someone being thoroughly taken in and enslaved by sin and darkness.

Let's take a look at Samson and how the spirit of seduction captivated him:

> "Now Samson went to Gaza and saw a harlot there, and went in to her. When the Gazites were told, 'Samson has come here!' they surrounded the place and lay in wait for him all night at the gate of the city. They were quiet all night, saying, 'In the morning, when it is daylight, we will kill him.' And Samson lay low till midnight; then he arose at midnight, took hold of the doors of the gate of the city and the two gateposts, pulled them up, bar and all, put them on his shoulders, and carried them to the top of the hill that faces Hebron.
>
> "Afterward it happened that he loved a woman in the Valley of Sorek, whose name was Delilah. And the Lords of the Philistines came up to her and said to her, 'Entice him, and find out where his great strength lies, and by what means we may overpower him, that we may bind him to afflict him; and every one of us will give you eleven hundred pieces of silver.'
>
> "So Delilah said to Samson, 'Please tell me where your great strength lies and with what you may be bound to afflict you.'
>
> "And Samson said to her, 'If they bind me with seven fresh bowstrings, not yet dried, then I shall become weak, and be like any other man.'
>
> "So the Lords of the Philistines brought up to her seven fresh bowstrings, not yet dried, and she bound

him with them. Now men were lying in wait, staying with her in the room. And she said to him, 'The Philistines are upon you, Samson!' But he broke the bowstrings as a strand of yarn breaks when it touches fire. So the secret of his strength was not known.

"Then Delilah said to Samson, 'Look, you have mocked me and told me lies. Now, please tell me what you may be bound with.'

"So he said to her, 'If they bind me securely with new ropes that have never been used, then I shall become weak, and be like any other man.'

"Therefore Delilah took new ropes and bound him with them, and said to him, 'The Philistines are upon you, Samson!' And men were lying in wait, staying in the room. But he broke them off his arms like a thread.

"Delilah said to Samson, 'Until now you have mocked me and told me lies. Tell me what you may be bound with.'

"And he said to her, 'If you weave the seven locks of my head into the web of the loom—"

"So she wove it tightly with the batten of the loom, and said to him, 'The Philistines are upon you, Samson!'

"But he awoke from his sleep, and pulled out the batten and the web from the loom.

"Then she said to him, 'How can you say, 'I love you,' when your heart is not with me? You have mocked me these three times, and have not told me where your great strength lies.'

"And it came to pass, when she pestered him daily with her words and pressed him so that his soul was vexed to death, that he told her all his heart, and said to her, 'No razor has ever come upon my head, for I have been a Nazirite to God from my mother's womb. If I am shaven, then my strength will leave me, and I shall become weak, and be like any other man.'

"When Delilah saw that he had told her all his heart, she sent and called for the Lords of the Philistines, saying, 'Come up once more, for he has told me all his heart.'

"So the Lords of the Philistines came up to her and brought the money in their hand. Then she lulled him to sleep on her knees, and called for a man and had him shave off the seven locks of his head. Then she began to torment him and his strength left him. And she said, 'The Philistines are upon you, Samson!'

"So he awoke from his sleep, and said, 'I will go out as before, at other times, and shake myself free!' But he did not know that the Lord had departed from him.

"Then the Philistines took him and put out his eyes, and brought him down to Gaza. They bound him with bronze fetters, and he became a grinder in the prison. However, the hair of his head began to grow again after it had been shaven." (Judges 16:1-22, NKJV).

THE DELILAH SYNDROME

Delilah represents the things in our lives that appear to be pleasing and desirable but have the potential to be deadly. Samson fell to the temptation of the enemy by hanging out with the one person who had the ability to cause him to desire wrong things.

"Do not be deceived: 'Evil company corrupts good habits.'" (1 Corinthians 15:33, NKJV).

It didn't take the entire Philistine army to take Samson down—just one person operating under the spirit of seduction. Satan can do the same thing using the spirit of seduction. Samson's strength came supernaturally from God and had little to do with his hair; it had to do with his relationship with God. When the kingdom of darkness succeeded in severing that relationship, Samson lost his strength, his sight, and his power. When we give into seduction and temptation, the price we must pay is usually very high, costing us our dignity and value in Christ.

As believers, we are called to be sold out to God. We live *in* the world, but we are not to be *of* the world. Samson wasn't sold out to God. He was in the world, and unfortunately, he was of the world as well. Because he didn't set himself apart—which was his calling from birth (Judges 13:5)—he was powerless to overcome the spirit of seduction. He had no scruples and no guilt about lying to the woman he said he loved; he even seemed to enjoy toying with her.

His relationship with God had become so damaged that he didn't realize that the power of God had left him after Delilah had cut his hair. When we fall victim to the spirit of seduction, we too often fail to realize that God's spirit is leaving us.

But just as Samson's power returned to him, even after he betrayed his calling, we can see God's power restored in our lives as well. We can recapture the power to defeat this evil spirit and bring glory to God.

RECOGNIZING THE SPIRIT OF SEDUCTION

The spirit of seduction can come through an individual or a group and is not gender specific. In the church, it's not always sexual; but regardless of how it manifests, it needs to be exposed and removed, so you don't end up in the helpless condition Samson found himself in after the seducing spirit had hooked him.

Here are five evidences of the people who are under a spirit of seduction:

1. They have silver tongues.

    There is a difference between flattery and a compliment. Both involve praise and adoration, but flattery is *empty* praise and adoration. It's used to manipulate and gain control or access to a person. People under the spirit of seduction will often flatter now for a payback later while the one who gives a compliment is usually sincere with their words of encouragement. Pray for discernment that you are not deceived.

    "Help, Lord; for the godly man ceaseth; for the faithful fail from among the children of men. They speak vanity every one with his neighbour: with flattering lips and with a double heart do they speak. The Lord shall cut off all flattering lips, and the tongue that speaketh proud things." (Psalm 12:1-3).

2. They refuse your refusal.

   The Bible gives us a perfect example of this in the story of Joseph and Potiphar's wife (Genesis 39). Women of character and renown were named in the Bible, but Potiphar's wife remained nameless and shameless. Potiphar's wife wanted to carry on a sexual relationship with her husband's servant Joseph, who knew it was wrong and refused her advances. Joseph reminded Potiphar's wife that her husband gave him charge of everything because Potiphar trusted him, and he refused to violate Potiphar's trust by sleeping with her. Joseph knew the spirit of seduction was wicked: "How then can I do this great wickedness and sin against God?" (Genesis 39:9).

   Every day this treacherous woman put the moves on Joseph, but he stood strong in his faith. As she continued to refuse his refusal, a day came when Joseph and Potiphar's wife were alone in the house. In another desperate attempt to seduce him, she grabbed his garment, and as Joseph tore himself away fleeing her grasp, his garment was left behind in her hands.

   He might have left without physical clothes, but he was still clothed with righteousness.

   You've heard it said that hell hath no fury like a woman scorned, and this is the perfect description of how Potiphar's wife reacted to Joseph's escape. She lied to her husband, telling him that Joseph came in to mock her and tried to sleep with her.

   People operating under the spirit of seduction want what they want at any cost, and they will make those who refuse them pay for their rejection. Potiphar's wife wanted what she wanted; Joseph rejected her; and she made Joseph pay a high price for dismissing her, convincing Potiphar to throw him into prison.

Just as they did in the time of Joseph, seducing spirits operate the same way today. We have to be mindful of who we allow into positions of leadership; while we may be impressed with their gifts or what they bring to the ministry, their hearts may be far from the will of God. When we refuse an idea or action, do they throw a temper tantrum? Make veiled threats? Go behind our back?

Pay attention and dismiss people who have the spirit of seduction, regardless of the price.

3. They play mind games.

Face it; to get their desired reaction from you, people will try to manipulate you with words, actions, pouting, fear, crying, guilt, sob stories, half-truths, and other subtle or not-so-subtle methods designed to control you and force you to change your mind. Although the Bible doesn't specifically spell out that manipulation is witchcraft, many Bible scholars believe that three kinds of witchcraft afflict Christians: intimidation, manipulation, and domination.

Consider the story of the well-educated woman who, as a babe in Christ, began dating a preacher. The preacher thought she was the smartest and prettiest woman on earth. He liked the fact that she was a business woman with many accolades, and she had an excellent reputation. She was college educated, and she possessed a sound financial mind. The preacher was her biggest fan until they married. But that's when everything changed.

From the first day they were married, the preacher became a man that the woman would describe as a street angel but a house devil. Every time she made a decision, no matter how insignificant, he would condemn her for not being submissive to him. She was no longer permitted to talk with her mother unless he was listening in on the extension. She was forbidden from going to the store to buy groceries without his supervision. Over time, he subtly manipulated her family and friends until they no longer talked to her, and soon he had her right where he wanted her—alone with only him in her life.

She would try to escape from her prison of loneliness, and she told him she made a mistake and wanted out. Every time she did, he would figuratively beat her over the head with Scripture. He would hurl threats at her about how God would retaliate against her if she divorced him.

"God will not be mocked!" he would yell. "You made a vow, and you cannot go back on your word to God. A three-fold cord is not easily broken, and you can't leave; it's not an option!"

This preacher had a Doctor of Divinity degree from a well-known, well-respected Christian university, and she was a baby Christian who lacked discernment on how he had twisted the Scriptures to manipulate her and controlled her emotions and actions. He would tell her repeatedly that there was no remission of willful sin, so she wouldn't go to heaven if she divorced him. She felt trapped and miserable, and she begged

God to take her life because, in death, she could be free from the spiritual abuse she lived with every day. She even began to hope that she would get a deadly disease to escape the prison she knew as marriage.

Eventually, she mustered the courage to leave the preacher and return to her family home, but not without the intense fear that God would punish her. She prayed every day and asked God to forgive her because the preacher had convinced her that she was weak for leaving him. He stalked her, harassed her by phone, issued threats, and improperly used the Bible as a weapon in an effort to regain control over her life and force her to return to him.

The pastor of the church this woman attended received threats from her husband as he tried to bully, manipulate, intimidate, and shame the pastor for counseling her to get a divorce and leave him. Her husband even convinced her that if she ever remarried, she would be responsible for sending her new husband to hell because they would be committing adultery, and she stayed single for many years because of his lies.

Over time, she began to heal, and she learned how to hold her own when he tried to manipulate her and how to rightly divide the Word of Truth. When his threats no longer had the desired impact, he stopped contacting her. It was a long haul from the days of abuse by a man operating with the spirit of seduction to the peace that passes all understanding. And in many ways, she was never able to return to the previous joy she knew as a babe in Christ, even though she had removed herself from the seducing spirit.

Manipulation should never be part of a believer's life. Whenever we find ourselves involved in manipulation, we must quickly repent and ask God to forgive us. And if you sense you are being manipulated, ask God to give you discernment and wisdom to handle the situation. We can avoid being manipulated by arming ourselves with the Word of God. When Satan tried to play mind games with Jesus, he always fought back with Scripture. And that's what we need to do too!

4. They are self-esteem junkies.

God hates pride because it causes us to think more highly of ourselves than we ought. When we fall victim to this self-centered attitude, we put ourselves above God and His Kingdom. Pride is what got Lucifer kicked out of heaven.

"How you are fallen from heaven,
O Lucifer, son of the morning!
How you are cut down to the ground,
You who weakened the nations!
For you have said in your heart:
'I will ascend into heaven,
I will exalt my throne above the stars of God;
I will also sit on the mount of the congregation
On the farthest sides of the north;
I will ascend above the heights of the clouds,
I will be like the Most High.'
Yet you shall be brought down to Sheol,
To the lowest depths of the Pit.
—Isaiah 14:12-15

When Satan attempted to exalt himself higher than God, God made things perfectly clear about who ruled the universe.

The spirit of seduction uses pride to keep many people from being saved, healed, and delivered. Pride is sinful because we give ourselves credit for things that are only possible with God. Some prideful people are loud, out front, obnoxious people while others are actually quite shy. Shy pride people may not sing on the worship team; may not teach a class; may choose not to pray when asked. They simply won't do anything. Why? Believe it or not, shyness can be a way for them to keep the focus on themselves, which is the very definition of pride.

"The wicked, through the pride of his countenance, will not seek after God: God is not in all his thoughts. His ways are always grievous; thy judgments are far above out of his sight: as for all his enemies, he puffeth at them. He hath said in his heart, I shall not be moved: for I shall never be in adversity." (Psalm 10:4-6).

5. They love the pressure cooker

The spirit of seduction uses pressure. It will put you in its pressure cooker and watch you boil.

"For we wrestle not against flesh and blood, but against principalities, against powers, against the rulers of the darkness of this world, against spiritual wickedness in high places." (Ephesians 6:12).

We are all in a spiritual battle, and the only way to fight a spiritual battle is with the use of spiritual weapons (2 Corinthians 10:4). We cannot win the battle against the spirit of seduction (or any other spirit) in our own strength. Only through the power of Christ that dwells in us can we overcome.

The spirit of seduction is at work in our churches and our ministries, so we must guard our hearts. And when we face with this spirit, don't tolerate it, obliterate it.

CHAPTER 9

THE SPIRIT OF JUDAS

"Then one of the twelve, called Judas Iscariot, went unto the chief priests, and said unto them, 'What will ye give me, and I will deliver him unto you?' And they covenanted with him for thirty pieces of silver. And from that time he sought opportunity to betray him."
—Matthew 26:14-16

Some of the most disgraceful and despicable people in history were traitors, and perhaps one of the most infamous of all time was Judas Iscariot, who betrayed Jesus for thirty pieces of silver from the chief priests. He even identified Jesus to the Roman soldiers with the kiss of death. Unlike most of us, Jesus expected Judas to betray him and knew it was going to happen. "And he answered and said, 'He that dippeth his hand with me in the dish, the same shall betray me.'" (Matthew 26:23).

Have you ever known anyone named Judas? Very few parents name their sons Judas because of the stigma attached to it. In fact, from 1880 to 2014, there were only a few hundred children given the name out of millions born during that time. The name is simply rarely used, but the meaning of the name hasn't changed since the days when Jesus walked the earth. Merriam-Webster and many other dictionaries give the meaning of Judas as a traitor, especially one who betrays under the guise of friendship. Even in the Bible, Judas is named last among the disciples and then usually with some negative comment added such as, "And Judas Iscariot, who betrayed him." (Matthew 10:4).

Earlier, we discussed the spirit of Absalom, and how that led to the betrayal of Absalom against his father, King David. Even David's closest friend, Ahithophel, joined in Absalom's plot. Although he befriended David, Ahithophel wanted to kill David because he was Bathsheba's grandfather, and he didn't like how David handled his adulterous affair with Bathsheba (2 Samuel 17).

Adam and Eve walked in the cool of the evening with God, and yet they betrayed Him. The serpent fed them a bill of goods that they could be like God if they ate the forbidden fruit, and they bought it (Genesis 3:4-5).

History records grievous betrayals, but history is still being written. The spirit of Judas is alive and well in the world, our churches, and our homes. The New Testament warns us of this in the last days. "And the brother shall deliver up the brother to death, and the father the child: and the children shall rise up against their parents, and cause them to be put to death." (Matthew 10:21).

Here are some characteristics of the spirit of Judas to watch out for:

1. It is often within our inner circle.

   Judas was one of the twelve disciples. He sat with Jesus, learned from Jesus, ate with Jesus, and was the treasurer of Jesus' ministry. When Jesus said that one of them would betray Him, no one considered Judas because he was trusted. In Matthew 6:70, Jesus answered a disciple's question by saying, "Have I not chosen you twelve, and one of you is a devil?"

2. It is often a lover of money.

   Judas was the treasurer and sold Jesus for thirty pieces of silver. Money was more appealing than protecting his friend Jesus. The enemy knew his weakness and hooked him. His love of money was stronger than his love for Jesus. The value of the thirty pieces of silver is estimated as five or six months' wages in Jesus' time, not very much considering Jesus could get coins out of fish mouths!

3. It is selfish.

   When the woman poured oil on Jesus from the alabaster box, Judas got upset. He accused the woman of being wasteful. Jesus straightforwardly rebuked Judas, saying, "Let her alone; she has kept this for the day of My burial (John 12:7, Holman Christian Standard Bible).

4. It is jealous of others.

   Peter, James, and John were a part of Jesus' inner circle. They witnessed more miracles than any of the other disciples. John was thought to be 'the disciple whom Jesus loved.'

5. The Devil follows the spirit of Judas.

 Judas betrayed Jesus when Satan entered him.

 "Then entered Satan into Judas surnamed Iscariot, being of the number of the twelve. And he went his way, and communed with the chief priests and captains, how he might betray him unto them. And they were glad, and covenanted to give him money." (Luke 22: 3–5).

6. It looks for like-minded allies.

 Judas was in cahoots with the chief priests and brought a group of soldiers to arrest Jesus. He created a show of strength, perhaps to make himself feel more powerful and important.

Nothing breaks our hearts more than betrayal, and it often leaves scars only God can heal. Once we have been betrayed, it is hard to trust again. Pain on the inside often leads to shame on the outside. Betrayal can feel like our hearts has been ripped from our chests. We can't explain the pain and hurt it causes, and we are left with a feeling of shock and disbelief.

We need to beware and be aware! We must take notice of those we allow into our inner circle and those we confide in. When a staff member requires correction, we should take note of those who rebel against leadership and correction. If they choose to walk out, let them go, and don't attempt to bring them back into the fold without covering them in prayer. Like Absalom, they could harbor a grudge, and they may be waiting for the right time to get even or cause us embarrassment and loss.

I've seen cases where disgruntled staff members have left a ministry to start their own church, causing a divide and even stealing money from the ministry unbeknownst to their leaders. Instead of repenting and seeking forgiveness from those they hurt, they doubled-down as they tried to damage the church, preferring to destroy rather than repair a ministry. We need to be very careful when picking our staff. Pray about each member and listen for the Holy Spirit's guidance.

We are all guilty of betrayal at some point. We need to repent to the Lord and ask for forgiveness from those we have betrayed.

CHAPTER 10

THE SPIRIT OF DISCORD

Blessed are the peacemakers:
for they shall be called the children of God.
—Matthew 5-9

We need to look no further than our church pews to understand that discord and divisiveness are real. These actions don't come from the Spirit of God.

Those who sow discord and strife sow seeds of bitterness, anger, and distrust in the soil of the hearts of others. People who stir up trouble and confusion are often insecure and are driven by their own personal agenda. They play on people's emotions, derive pleasure from creating conflict, and drama follows them wherever they go. They are typically spiritual babies because spiritual maturity won't begin until the drama ends. Sometimes they know what they're doing, but the spirit of discord has such a hold on them that they just play right into the hands of spiritual forces whose only objective is to destroy the mission of the church or ministry. Sometimes, the spirit of discord feeds on the behavior of these spiritual babies by reminding them of their past injuries and failures while also creating doubts about their future. Those under the influence of the spirit of discord are almost always filled with a great sense of inner turmoil.

The spirit of discord seeks out the vulnerabilities in others, looking for weaknesses in their emotions and feelings. A person under its influence will exploit those weaknesses, offering the appearance of "one called alongside to help"—Parakletos in Greek, usually referring to the Holy Spirit—but instead they provide nothing constructive or helpful. They divide God's people instead of bringing them together. When a person projects anger and hostility to members of the Body of Christ, especially the leaders, it is often the result of being under the influence of the spirit of discord.

People afflicted with the spirit of discord are rarely lone wolves, so they work on building a group of followers to increase their influence and make them appear stronger than they really are. Unfortunately, the body is so full of spiritual babes in Christ that they are usually quite successful in finding someone willing to join their cause. The spirit of discord creates masters of manipulation; able to twist the negative emotions, lies, half-truths and innuendos of the vulnerable into dishonest personal gain. It's one of the reasons we need to always guard our hearts (Proverbs 4:23) because our fleshly old nature will almost always find bad news a tad more exciting than good news.

> "A naughty person, a wicked man, walketh with a froward mouth. He winketh with his eyes, he speaketh with his feet, he teacheth with his fingers; Frowardness is in his heart, he deviseth mischief continually; he soweth discord. Therefore shall his calamity come suddenly; suddenly shall he be broken without remedy.

"These six things doth the Lord hate: yea, seven are an abomination unto him: A proud look, a lying tongue, and hands that shed innocent blood, An heart that deviseth wicked imaginations, feet that be swift in running to mischief, A false witness that speaketh lies, and he that soweth discord among brethren." (Proverbs 6:12-19).

As the old saying goes, it's as plain as the nose on your face. Unfortunately, many or all of these are often found in the same person under the influence of the spirit of discord. Look for these signs:

1. Lack of love.

   When love for others is lacking, we may act selfishly; treating others unfairly or callously while justifying our negative behavior.

   "Hatred stirs up strife: but love covers all sins." (Proverbs 10:12).

2. Lack of contentment.

   When we are not content with what God has given us and done for us, we become dissatisfied with nearly everything.

   "But Godliness with contentment is great gain, for we brought nothing into the world, and we cannot take anything out of the world. But if we have food and clothing, with these we will be content." (1 Timothy 6:6-8).

3. Lack of self-control.

Those who are Kingdom-minded do not have time to sow the seeds of discord. One of the ways the Bible describes the person lacking self-control is as a busybody.

"But let none of you suffer as a murderer, or as a thief, or as an evildoer, or as a busybody in other men's matters. (1 Peter 4:15).

4. Lack of peace.

Uncontrolled emotions, fits of rage, angry outbursts, and a quarrelsome nature are signs that the spirit of discord is working. This lack of peace can lead to divisions that last long after the initial outburst.

"Surely the churning of milk bringeth forth butter, and the wringing of the nose bringeth forth blood: so the forcing of wrath bringeth forth strife." (Proverbs 30:33).

5. Lack of good will.

When we lack the ability to show good will towards others, we become envious, jealous and selfish.

"For where jealousy and selfish ambition exist, there is disorder and every evil thing." (James 3:16).

6. Lack of humility.

Arrogance and pride have brought many men to ruin and shame. A proud person refuses to admit when they are wrong and almost always rejects opposing viewpoints. Prideful people operate with an over-inflated sense of importance, and, by comparison, consider others to be of lesser value. Pride and stubbornness lead to conflict.

"He that is of a proud heart stirreth up strife: but he that putteth his trust in the Lord shall be made fat." (Proverbs 28:25).

While the spirit of discord is always destructive, there are four behaviors that are particularly destructive to interpersonal relationships; causing division in the church:

1. Being judgmental of others.

Matthew 7:1-2 tells us, "Judge not, that ye be not judged. For with what judgment ye judge, ye shall be judged: and with what measure ye mete, it shall be measured to you again."

When Jesus was praying in the garden, he asked the Father for his followers to operate in a spirit of unity to prove to the world that He was sent by God (John 17:20-23). One of the best ways to do this is to avoid being judgmental. Unfortunately, many of us fall short from time-to-time, but nothing will destroy a relationship or a church quicker than being judgmental. While we are also commanded to rightly divide the truth (2 Timothy 2:15), those with the spirit of discord will judge others harshly, making everyone subject to their scrutiny.

"But why dost thou judge thy brother? or why dost thou set at nought thy brother? For we shall all stand before the judgment seat of Christ." (Romans 14:10).

Because we are all sinners, the world would be a better place if we stopped dwelling on the failings of others and started attending to our own serious issues. The Bible is plain about it: "Thou hypocrite, first cast out the beam out of thine own eye; and then shalt thou see clearly to cast out the mote out of thy brother's eye." (Matthew 7:5).

We should make every effort to be merciful, kind, and patient in our dealings with others as we let God be the judge.

2. Speaking evil of others.

As we learned earlier about the spirit of gossip, the out-of-control tongue can do more damage than a nuclear bomb! Harsh, hateful and slanderous statements about others will often proceed from of the mouths of those with the spirit of discord. The tongue has the power to deliver life or death to the spirit of another.

"But the tongue can no man tame; it is an unruly evil, full of deadly poison. Therewith bless we God, even the Father; and therewith curse we men, which are made after the similitude of God. Out of the same mouth proceedeth blessing and cursing. My brethren, these things ought not so to be." (James 3:8-10).

3. Attacking the character of others.

Differences with our brothers and sisters in Christ will happen from time-to-time. Even Paul, the author of much of the New Testament, had such a sharp disagreement with one of the early leaders of the church

(Barnabas) that they decided to part company with each going his own way (Acts 15:39). When we have a problem with someone, God's Word tells us exactly how to deal with it. When we have *ought* with someone (as the King James Version describes it), we are instructed to go to the person who wronged us in secret. That is sometimes hard to do, but it gets the problem out in the open and allows two Christian people to work it out in love without an audience chiming in.

If we do this, and the person refuses to reconcile, we can get others involved. God's way is to get two or more witnesses; if they still refuse, take it to the church; and if they reject the church, let them go and avoid them. We can't keep people around who operate in the spirit of discord and refuse correction. They will divide our church and ministry.

"Moreover if thy brother shall trespass against thee, go and tell him his fault between thee and him alone: if he shall hear thee, thou hast gained thy brother. But if he will not hear thee, then take with thee one or two more, that in the mouth of two or three witnesses every word may be established. And if he shall neglect to hear them, tell it unto the church: but if he neglect to hear the church, let him be unto thee as an heathen man and a publican." (Matthew 18: 15-17).

4. Being unforgiving of others.

Forgiveness is one of the hardest things in the world to do. The pain we experience when people do us wrong—intentionally or not—can last a lifetime if we let it. It's not easy to forgive someone who hurt us or made us mad. We want to see them pay for causing us pain instead of forgiving them. We want to get even, but God commands us to forgive—not just once, but repeatedly:

"Then came Peter to him, and said, Lord, how oft shall my brother sin against me, and I forgive him? Till seven times? Jesus saith unto him, I say not unto thee, until seven times: but, until seventy times seven." (Matthew 18: 21-22).

Four hundred ninety times? Really? Actually, I think what Jesus was telling us is that He wants us to show *unlimited* Christian character and grace to others. And guess what, if we don't forgive others, our Heavenly Father won't forgive us. I'm not sure about you, but I would hate to stand before Jesus someday and be denied forgiveness because I held something petty (or even significant) against someone.

"For if ye forgive men their trespasses, your heavenly Father will also forgive you. But if ye forgive not men their trespasses, neither will your Father forgive your trespasses." (Matthew 6:14-15).

Unforgiveness destroys relationships, churches, and ministries, but it can also destroy our health. Studies have shown that it can increase muscle tension, causing headaches and other types of body aches. It can decrease blood flow which deprives every part of the body of oxygen and nutrition, and it makes it more difficult for our bodies to eliminate toxins which can cause organ failure. It can affect our sleep, impair our body's ability to recover from injury, cause ulcers, and even lead to heart attacks.

Even if we have trouble forgiving others for their sakes, we should forgive others for our health's sake. Scripture tells us in 2 John 1:2, "Beloved, I wish above all things that thou mayest prosper and be in health, even as thy soul prospereth."

5. We have to turn discord into concord.

   "Ye have heard that it hath been said, Thou shalt love thy neighbour, and hate thine enemy. But I say unto you, love your enemies, bless them that curse you, do good to them that hate you, and pray for them which despitefully use you, and persecute you." (Matthew 5: 43-44).

6. We need to stop majoring in minors.

   "And the servant of the Lord must not strive; but be gentle unto all men, apt to teach, patient, in meekness instructing those that oppose themselves; if God peradventure will give them repentance to the acknowledging of the truth; And that they may recover themselves out of the snare of the devil, who are taken captive by him at his will." (Timothy 2:24-26).

   Listen to the still small voice of the Holy Spirit, and He will guide us on how to confront, correct, and inspire.

CHAPTER 11

THE SPIRIT OF OFFENSE

"And then shall many be offended,
and shall betray one another, and shall hate one
another. And many false prophets shall rise, and shall
deceive many. And because iniquity shall abound,
the love of many shall wax cold. But he that shall
endure unto the end, the same shall be saved."
—Matthew 24:10-13

The day Matthew spoke about has arrived. The world today is full of offended people. Some are offended by the pastor and leave the church. In the workplace, employees get offended and leave their jobs. Husbands are offended by their wives and wives by their husbands, resulting in some of the highest divorce rates in history. Friends get offended with each other and end their friendships. Even children get offended. Today, people wake up with attitudes; they are mad, angry, and easily offended.

Merriam-Webster's online dictionary defines *offense* as being insulted or morally outraged; a stumbling block and cause or occasion for sin. Brothers and sisters under the influence of the spirit of offense choke out conversations, refuse to give the benefit of the doubt, are intolerant, and almost always assume the worst. It causes us to blame others while preventing us from accepting responsibility for our actions. Always looking for the ugly, this spirit breeds dissatisfaction and hurt feelings.

Let's be honest, we all have had our feelings hurt, have been treated unfairly, and have felt victimized. If we allow those feeling to turn into anger and hang on to it, the spirit of offense can take root, causing us to fall into Satan's trap. When that happens, we are held back from God's blessings in our lives. We have to resolve the issue, and if we can't, we have to let go and let God.

Many times an offense between members of the Body is caused by miscommunication. Someone says or does something, and we interpret it through a filter of weak emotions or unhealed wounds. When we get our feelings hurt in this manner, we lose our objectivity and take offense. If we want to break the spirit of offense, we have to ignore harsh words, resolve ourselves to forgive, and release the resentment we might be feeling.

Practice makes perfect. Often we choose to be offended, and the more often we make that choice, the easier it is to be upset about every little thing. However, if we choose to forgive others and release the resentment, it will become a habit and cause us to walk in the Spirit daily while we kill the desires of the flesh (Galatians 5:16).

Notice I said *choose*. How we respond to the spirit of offense is always a choice; we don't have to be offended. We can choose to refuse offense.

I know a couple who have been happily married for more than forty years. Like all of us, they have bad days, but they have a rule that they have followed from the first day of their marriage. They agreed never to let the sun go down on their anger (Ephesians 4:26). If one of them is offended or angry, the other must remain calm and refuse to get mad as the offended partner airs any grievances with the other. When the offended person is finished, they agree to look for solutions and cover the problem with prayer. They agree to avoid raising their voices, showing irritation, or acting negatively in any way. If necessary, they have stayed up all night to avoid going to bed angry.

This couple understands that it is normal to get irritated sometimes, and they recognize that offenses will occur because they are human. But by acting calmly when the other person isn't as calm, this couple has never had a serious fight. They work together to fix any problem that arises.

If we hang on to offense, it will fester like an open wound. It will cause us to lose our joy and rob us of fellowship with the Body of Christ. In fact, Jesus is so serious about not letting offenses build up that He doesn't even want our offerings if we hold onto offense. We must always try to mend our differences with those who have offended us.

"Therefore if thou bring thy gift to the altar, and there rememberest that thy brother hath ought against thee; Leave there thy gift before the altar, and go thy way; first be reconciled to thy brother, and then come and offer thy gift." (Matthew 5:23-24).

The spirit of offense is made worse when we choose to dwell on past hurts caused by abusive parents, relationships, and spouses. When we find ourselves in this condition, we need to turn those hurts over to God and move on; it's the only way we can be all we were created to be. God can—if we let him—heal and remove those hurts before they destroy us and our ministries. As I mentioned earlier, forgiveness is a choice, and it should never be handled based on our emotions or how we might "feel" at the time.

It's been said that hurt people hurt people. What does that mean? In a nutshell, it means that the person who hurts others has himself/herself been hurt. If we keep that in mind as we deal with forgiving those who have offended us, it becomes easier to forgive them, knowing that they have hurts of their own. It can also help us be more forgiving because, if we hold on to the hurt of offense, we will become offenders ourselves; operating under the spirit of offense. Nursing this spirit and hanging onto offenses sets us up for frustration, bitterness, depression, and all that comes with it.

CHAPTER 12

THE SPIRIT OF CAIN

"Not as Cain, who was of that wicked one,
and slew his brother. And wherefore slew he him?
Because his own works were evil,
and his brother's righteous."
—1 John 3:12

The spirit of Cain is a murdering spirit, and tragically, is alive and well today. When Cain saw that God accepted his brother Abel's offering and did not accept his, Cain envied the blessing on Abel's life. Anger rose within Cain, and his anger culminated and in a fit of rage, he murdered his own brother.

God rejected Cain's offering, but he did not reject Cain. On the other hand, God accepted Abel's offering. "By faith Abel offered unto God a more excellent sacrifice than Cain, by which he obtained witness that he was righteous, God testifying of his gifts: and by it he being dead yet speaketh." (Hebrews 11:4).

Scripture doesn't tell us if Cain or Abel knew ahead of time if their offerings would be pleasing to God, and we don't know if God required a blood sacrifice, even the Scriptural account does seem to point us in that direction. Perhaps the rejection of Cain's offering had more to do with him than his offering. What we do know is that God is sovereign over His creation, and there are times when we must acknowledge that "His thoughts are not our thoughts, and His ways are not our ways." (Isaiah 55:8).

Although there are numerous denominations throughout the world, human history has seen only two actual forms of religion: Abel's religion of Grace received by faith, and Cain's religion of works without grace.

Under the religion of Abel, we are able to understand the gift of Jesus Christ because He was the Lamb "slain from the foundation of the world" (Revelation 13:8) for our redemption as He took the curse of the world upon himself (Galatians 3:13).

The spirit of Cain rejects the work of Christ, leaning instead on the appearance of holiness. Under Cain, Christ's sacrifice on the cross is replaced by self-centered works. The supernatural is replaced with earthly treasures where moths and vermin destroy and where thieves break in and steal (Matthew 6:19, NIV).

People under the influence of the spirit of Cain display weak character. They are self-centered individuals looking for affirmation and attention from others. And when they don't get it, they become destructive, even murderous (spiritually speaking). They are spiritually immature and unaccountable.

We need to be on the lookout for the spirit of Cain in these last days. Jude 1:11-19 tells us how it will manifest itself in the last days.

> "Woe unto them! for they have gone in the way of Cain, and ran greedily after the error of Balaam for reward, and perished in the gainsaying of Core. These

> are spots in your feasts of charity, when they feast with you, feeding themselves without fear: clouds they are without water, carried about of winds; trees whose fruit withereth, without fruit, twice dead, plucked up by the roots; Raging waves of the sea, foaming out their own shame; wandering stars, to whom is reserved the blackness of darkness forever. And Enoch also, the seventh from Adam, prophesied of these, saying, Behold, the Lord cometh with ten thousands of his saints, To execute judgment upon all, and to convince all that are ungodly among them of all their ungodly deeds which they have ungodly committed, and of all their hard speeches which ungodly sinners have spoken against him. These are murmurers, complainers, walking after their own lusts; and their mouth speaketh great swelling words, having men's persons in admiration because of advantage. But, beloved, remember ye the words which were spoken before of the apostles of our Lord Jesus Christ; How that they told you there should be mockers in the last time, who should walk after their own ungodly lusts. These be they who separate themselves, sensual, having not the Spirit."

Repent! Turn away! Unless there is absolute repentance, people with the spirit of Cain will live with the mark for the rest of their lives. Don't follow those who walk in this spirit. They are headed for destruction and hardship. Their murderous spirits will eventually kill your momentum and your spirit.

CHAPTER 13

THE SPIRIT OF WITCHCRAFT

"Beloved, believe not every spirit,
but try the spirits whether they are of God:
because many false prophets are
gone out into the world."
—1 John 4:1

In the Old Testament, those who dealt in witchcraft were condemned to death (Exodus 22:18). Why? Because the Devil often imitates the things of God, using witchcraft as a feeble substitute for true spirituality as he creates doubt and causes people to believe a lie. Weak Christians who have not put on the whole armor of God often aren't even aware that they are being led away from the things of God.

Many of our brothers and sisters in Christ fail to realize when the spirit of witchcraft is oppressing them because of the subtle way it surrounds them daily, appearing to almost be normal and acceptable.

I'm not necessarily talking about Ouija boards, casting spells, black magic, charms, pentagrams, tarot card readings, etc. Most Christians recognize these obvious tools of darkness. I'm talking about the subtle tools used by the enemy; the less obvious ways he attempts to undermine God's plan and God's family.

Taking illegal mind-altering drugs, reading daily horoscopes, and watching television shows and movies depicting sorcery and witchcraft are good examples of how the enemy tempts God's people. For example, millions of Christians from at least two continents read or watched the *Harry Potter* series with equal or greater enthusiasm than the *Left Behind* series, and didn't think twice about the witchcraft that entertained them. Is it possible that they made a place for the Devil without even realizing it?

Those under the influence of the spirit of witchcraft seek to control and manipulate people, circumstances, and events to get their own way. Instead of trusting God to guide them, they seize the reins of control from Him much like Eve did when the serpent beguiled her in the Garden of Eden. The spirit of witchcraft is a powerful tool in the enemy's toolbox, and it can infiltrate our churches before we realize it. And when we walk in the flesh, we are particularly prone to the destruction it can bring:

"Now the works of the flesh are manifest, which are these; Adultery, fornication, uncleanness, lasciviousness, idolatry, witchcraft, hatred, variance, emulations, wrath, strife, seditions, heresies, envyings, murders, drunkenness, revellings, and such like: of the which I tell you before, as I have also told you in time past, that they which do such things shall not inherit the kingdom of God." (Galatians 19 – 21).

RECOGNIZING AND DEALING WITH THE SPIRIT OF WITCHCRAFT

Rebellion is one sign that witchcraft is active. Saul rebelled against God when he went to destroy the Amalekites, and it cost him his kingdom. "For rebellion is as the sin of witchcraft, and stubbornness is as iniquity and idolatry. Because thou hast rejected the word of the Lord, he hath also rejected thee from being king." (1 Samuel 15:23).

Rebellion is always dangerous! When we find it in our church leadership, we must expose it and correct it. If left unabated, it can end up controlling and destroying us as well.

Along the same vein, if a member of our church body is a troublemaker who seeks to destroy the unity, harmony, and reputation of God's people, we must expose and correct them as well. Being a troublemaker is a manifestation of the spirit of witchcraft, and will create confusion when God desires the spirit of peace (1 Corinthians 14:33). If the spirit of witchcraft goes unchecked, it will leave destruction in its wake, especially with those in the pulpit.

I'm not saying that we need to surround ourselves with "Yes Men" or "Yes Women." It's important that we allow ourselves to be sharpened by the iron of others (Proverbs 27:17). When we learn to grow together, we can build God's vision for our lives together.

What I am saying is that there are those in the Body who aren't interested in working to build up others because they are more interested in building up themselves. They become so self-centered that they become self-destructive, and when they run out of ways to hurt themselves, they turn their attention on others.

Have you ever heard of spotlight Christians? These are people who believe that the world around them will fall apart if they're not in control. They think nothing can be done correctly without them right in the middle of it, and they will try to manipulate every situation to their advantage in order to control everyone and everything, bringing the focus back to themselves. They are high-minded, headstrong, overbearing, opinionated, uncaring, and not giving or forgiving.

We can never tolerate the spirit of witchcraft. It is a powerful spirit, and we need to attack early and often before it infiltrates our lives and our churches. A church under the influence of someone operating with the spirit of witchcraft will suffer from manipulation when it should be experiencing manifestation and revelation.

We need only to look to the story of Paul to gain the insight necessary to address the spirit of witchcraft: "And it came to pass, as we went to prayer, a certain damsel possessed with a spirit of divination met us, which brought her masters much gain by soothsaying: The same followed Paul and us, and cried, saying, 'These men are the servants of the most high God, which shew unto us the way of salvation.' And this did she many days. But Paul, being grieved, turned and said to the spirit, I command thee in the name of Jesus Christ to come out of her. And he came out the same hour." (Acts 15:16-18).

Paul was secure in who he was in Christ. He had a firm relationship with the Lord, and the demon in the damsel did not intimidate him one bit. He commanded the spirit to leave: No ifs, ands, buts, or "pretty please." Just a simple command because he knew his authority in Christ. The spirit knew Paul had authority, and so did the Devil.

IDENTIFYING THE SPIRIT OF WITCHCRAFT IN YOUR LIFE

The spirit of witchcraft will drain us of our energy, make us feel tired, and increase our stress level. It doesn't matter if we are perfectly healthy, exercise regularly, get plenty of sleep, take vitamins, or run a mile a day. The fatigue we can feel stems from being oppressed and influenced by the spirit world, not the physical world. Even when we are well-rested, our kids are behaving, our health is good, our bills are paid, and our marriages are harmonious, we can still feel stressed and exhausted—too weary for well doing. And that's exactly where the enemy wants us!

The Holy Spirit can't work where a controlling spirit takes up residence. The spirit of witchcraft is a hindrance to the work of faith. It overwhelms faith and leaves no room for faith to operate. The spirit of witchcraft takes the spotlight off God and puts it on us. We can't worship God when we are worshiping ourselves!

When the spirit of witchcraft rears its ugly head, humble yourself before God and seek His forgiveness. Then, using the authority of the name of Jesus Christ, remove the spirit of witchcraft from your life.

CONCLUSION

Jesus called the Devil the father of lies. In John 8:44, he said, "Ye are of your father the Devil, and the lusts of your father ye will do. He was a murderer from the beginning, and abode not in the truth, because there is no truth in him. When he speaketh a lie, he speaketh of his own: for he is a liar, and the father of it."

Spirits are real, both good and evil. God is a spirit, and the Devil operates from the spirit world. Ephesians 6:12 tells us, "For we wrestle not against flesh and blood, but against principalities, against powers, against the rulers of the darkness of this world, against spiritual wickedness in high places."

These powers operate inside the church. The more on fire a person is for God, the more spiritual warfare they are likely to encounter. When we are surrounded by challenges on all sides, the spirit world is usually battling behind the scenes. We need to be aware of the battles raging in our midst, and we need to take action to confront and stop the spirits that hinder and divide God's people. We are God's anointed. We are the watchmen for the Kingdom. It's our responsibility, as well as our privilege, to sound the alarm and protect our Christian brothers and sisters.

ABOUT THE AUTHOR

Dr. Ron Webb is the author of *Leadership from Behind the Scenes* and *Destroying the Root of Racism*. And he is the pastor of the Mt. Calvary Powerhouse Church in Poplar Bluff, Missouri. Pastor Webb has been in the ministry for over 30 years. He attended Three Rivers Community College in Poplar Bluff where he majored in Business Administration and was a former "Raider" basketball player. He earned his Bachelor of Theology degree from the International College of Bible Theology, and a Master Degree of Pastor Studies in Counseling, and a Doctorate of Theology from Midwest Theological Seminary. Dr. Webb also had the honor of doing the invocation at the inauguration of Missouri Governor Jay Nixon.

The unique ministry of Dr. Ron Webb is evident as he is anointed in the areas of church leadership and governance. Dr. Webb has been considered by many to be "A Pastor to Pastors." His ministry is centered on restoration and racial reconciliation and a sincere belief that we must teach the lost at any cost. His preaching and teaching focus on empowerment and hope.

Dr. Webb is CEO and President of *S.E.M.O. Christian Restoration Center*, a place for individuals who need a second chance in life. He is founder and lead instructor of *School of the Prophets Bible College* in Poplar Bluff, Missouri. Students leave this Bible college as trained and experienced leaders ready to fulfill Jesus' command in Matthew 28:19 to "go ye therefore, and teach all nations."

The *Heartland Family Center,* a homeless shelter for families, is an outreach ministry organized and founded in 2007 by Dr. Webb, and is owned and operated by Mt. Calvary Powerhouse Church. The goal is to serve families whose circumstances have deprived them of adequate living and housing. In a Christ-like manner, families in need are provided housing and services to help them become self-sufficient.

Covenant Ministries is another ministry designed by Dr. Webb to advance God's Kingdom by providing a fellowship in which men and women of God find mutual encouragement, edification, counsel, and participation in leadership and ministerial training.

Dr. Webb is married to the lovely Georgia Webb, and they have three children: Ronnie, Jr., Tony, and Jackie (Webb) Brown. Grandpa Ron and Grandma Georgia boast two grandchildren so far: Jerrell Brown, Jr. and Jaxson Brown.

CPSIA information can be obtained
at www.ICGtesting.com
Printed in the USA
LVOW04s1110010716
494917LV00001B/1/P